CASTLE
CATS

For Blanca, Carlos and Gabriel

CASTLE
CATS

Richard Surman

HarperCollins*Publishers*

HarperCollins*Publishers*
77-85 Fulham Palace Road, London W6 8JB

First published in Great Britain
in 1995 by HarperCollins*Publishers*

1 3 5 7 9 10 8 6 4 2

Copyright © 1995 Richard Surman

Richard Surman asserts the moral right to be
identified as the author and photographer of this work

A catalogue record for this book is
available from the British Library

0 00 627945-7

Printed and bound by Bath Press Colourbooks
Blantyre Glasgow

Contents

Introduction

The private life of cats is always the subject of speculation: their take-it or leave-it independence, mixed with an extraordinary sociability seems to intrigue humans, whose lives are constrained by convention. The cat is seen as a solitary animal. Rudyard Kipling's 'The Cat who walked by Himself' portrays the cat as a creature with no sense of territory. I don't think this is so. True, cats hunt by themselves and give every appearance of being beholden to no one, but these unique and special animals define for themselves, according to their own mysterious and idiosyncratic rules, the terms on which they cohabit with humans. As for having no sense of place, one only has to turn to the many tales of epic journeys made by cats determined to return to a favoured place to realize that they form deep territorial attachments.

I turned to cats in castles with slight trepidation, suspecting that castle inhabitants might be more 'doggish' than 'cattish'. However, I consoled myself with the thought that castles are for the most part very large, old and rambling and that, even in the face of stiff opposition from exuberant gun dogs, *felis catus* would have established a toehold. An iron grip might be a more suitable description of the cats' presence in many of the castles.

There are some distinct national variations. In Scotland the mere mention of cats in the presence of a ghillie is enough to induce barely suppressed rage. In England the situation is less tense, cats being actively encouraged for a variety of reasons ranging from an appreciation of their regal presence to the need for pest control. Cats in Ireland are drawn to castles as if by magnetism. Even where there is no particular interest shown in their presence, the cats still penetrate those castles in which they wish to live.

I've been tantalized by information of past cats and other animal life at the castles in Britain and Ireland. The Dowager Countess Cawdor told me that three Jack Russells kept feline interest in Cawdor Castle to a minimum, although there had once been a resident cat called Nippy; Abyssinian cats had been a feature of castle life at Raby Castle in Yorkshire. The Duke of Buccleuch and Queensberry, whilst not being able to offer a current cat, told me of the animal belonging to one of his ancestors, the third Earl of Southampton – you'll find this story in the section on the Tower of London; whilst Lord Courtenay wrote to me from Powderham Castle suggesting that, as they had no cats, but a large family of tortoises, I should write a book on Castle Tortoises! Liz O'Driscoll, of Castle Matrix in Ireland regaled me with tales of the family's cat, Harley (deceased). I visited Castle Matrix to observe at first hand the fruits of a long and patient campaign to encourage two feral cats into the castle. At the time I was there, the cats would come to feed under cover of darkness as far as a cottage, hard by the old castle walls.

A castle cat in the making

Doubtless there will come a day in the not too distant future when they'll move in. The cats of Penhow Castle replied personally to me, and were the only cats in the book to admit publicly to being literate.

The cat has, through history, inspired an extraordinary amount of attention, across cultures, and in widely differing contexts. Remains of cats have been uncovered in Neolithic settlements, whilst the cat has a well-documented association with humans in ancient Egypt. Roman settlers in Britain are known to have kept domestic cats, as did the Anglo-Saxons. How fortunate are the great castles to be graced by such courtly animals.

There are many people to whom I am extremely grateful for their assistance in helping me assemble this book: first and foremost, to all the cats' guardians, for allowing me to creep through the undergrowth, scale the walls, haunt the battlements, stalk the halls and stairways and generally behave rather curiously in pursuit of their cats; Peter Reekie, Head of Press Relations and Ann Clipson, Head of Design, both of the National Trust for Scotland, for their advice and for illustrations

of three of the Scottish castles; Irish Heritage Properties gave me some invaluable pointers as to the whereabouts of my Irish cats, even if their switchboard operator at first thought I was a practical joker.

The enthusiasm of my editor Giles Semper has made a major contribution to the book, as has the forbearance of his assistant Roz Webber, especially as I did nothing but 'phone her with disaster stories of missing cats, cancelled ferryboats, blizzards in the Scottish mountains and tree-blocked roads. Barbara Chapman, my desk editor, has again patiently kept me on the straight and narrow. I recently realized that none of them has a cat, a state of affairs I'm tempted to put right at Christmas.

Last but certainly not least I wish to thank my family. My two young sons, Carlos and Gabriel, took great pleasure in helping me select the illustrations (even if some of them were upside down) and serenaded me strenuously when the muse was elusive. My wife Blanca also helped with research, and her patience in enduring my constant travelling was not far short of angelic.

Tabitha

Tabitha's enigmatic fascination with funerals has everyone bewildered. The first funeral she attended was that of a notable local cat lover. Since then she has stolidly plodded along behind any funeral cortège, tail held high as if in honour of the departed spirit.

Tabitha hears the funeral bell

She has developed a more general interest in things of the spirit, attending various services and meetings at the parish church, and occasionally getting locked inside. This happened one Christmas: Tabitha was mighty relieved to be let out in time to sink her claws into the Christmas turkey.

She has always been a bit of a wanderer. Reeling from the shock of having had five kittens at the tender age of nine months, she strolled from her owner Mrs Robinson's house, to a neighbour, Kay Hayward. She clearly felt that she needed a bit of loving care, never mind the kittens. Mrs Hayward was quite happy to have Tabitha as a visitor, but the cat's routine was a bit unsettling, rising as she did at two-thirty each morning to indulge in the noisy and indescribable things cats do in the early hours.

An idle moment before the tearooms open

Tabitha also had the habit of sauntering out into the main street, bringing traffic to a screeching halt, whilst she sat and heedlessly washed her tail. One day an inconsiderate driver ran into her, causing injuries that by rights no living creature should have survived. Her recovery was complete, but she decided that, from then on, castle life would be much less hazardous. Indeed nearby Berkeley Castle has provided Tabitha with a cat's Elysium, not least because she has shrewdly engaged the affections of Jill Hammond, assistant to the castle custodian, and owner of Siamese, Burmese and Abyssinian cats.

The castle is built on a promontory of sandstone, standing over a series of beautifully gardened terraces. Its present appearance is almost magical, but the castle has always been a fortress first and family home second. Massively dominating the surrounding countryside, Berkeley features in Shakespeare, and was the scene of the gruesome murder of Edward II. Today one of its more intriguing but bizarre internal features is a deep stone pit, filled in past times with rotting carcasses. Prisoners were kept over it until they either expired from the foul vapours or were sent to join the unwholesome contents of the pit!

In spite of her churchgoing, Tabitha herself wreaks mass murder amongst the local squirrels, whose luckless corpses she flaunts in front of the local foxhounds, orchestrating their rising hysteria with a mischievous flick or two of her tail. She is quietly disdainful of all dogs. A cat who was born on a goat farm is never going to have too much trouble with them.

Unwittingly, she has embraced the castle's jealously guarded tradition. Its hounds at one time hunted across all the land from Gloucestershire to London. Tabitha

*Berkeley Castle's most diligent
guardian*

A cat that can match a cannon

can herself often be spotted streaking through the undergrowth after some hapless squirrel, and her look-out points from the various terraces and roof-tops would draw the admiration of any military mind.

One of her favourite vantage points is a roof that overlooks the entrance to the tearooms, and in the winter, when the castle is closed to visitors, Tabitha can often be seen morosely watching the door for some sign of activity. At Easter, when the tearooms open, she's the first in the queue. Discouraged from coming in, she nevertheless often manages a quick foray, retrieving the fragments of home-made scone to which she is particularly partial – but only with clotted cream. If the pickings outside are slim, she enters the castle by any number of different routes, inevitably setting of the alarms and being unceremoniously shooed out by the guides.

Cookie and Freddy

Freddy doesn't hail from Elsinore Castle but he
had only one thing on his mind when he came
to Eastnor Castle: Revenge!

Freddy takes his ease

Cookie's Freddy-free zone

The large and impudent mouse population of Eastnor Castle got quite a shock when Isabella, second-oldest daughter of James and Sarah Hervey-Bathurst, arrived back with a cat. She had picked out Cookie, a self-possessed and decorous lady cat, at a cat rescue centre nearby, watched in disbelief by Freddy, a large tom in the next enclosure. He was equally desperate for a home and convinced that he could be the only choice for anyone wanting a splendid cat.

It was worse that Cookie had spurned his extravagant advances. In fact she glanced with relief over her shoulder at him as she was whisked away, for Freddy had a rather inflated view of his own appeal. Luckily for

Freddy, Isabella's older sister, Imogen, couldn't get him out of her mind. After two days of beseeching she was allowed to fetch Freddy as a second castle cat. How could she have known that her actions would re-introduce two old adversaries?

Cookie was sitting engrossed in front of the renowned Meryck collection of medieval armour acquired by the third Earl in the late nineteenth century – by his own admission he had an acute case of 'armouritis' – when in walked Imogen, clasping a jubilant Freddy to her. Cookie must have thought herself to be dreaming. But the malevolent leer Freddy cast her way convinced her that this was no feline nightmare and she streaked for cover behind a nearby shield. The ensuing cat wars were worthy of a minstrel's attentions. The battles raged inside and out: the ferocious shrieks of the two cats reverberated through the castle, giving rise to the rumour that two banshees had taken up residence at the wrong castle.

Eastnor Castle, built in the early nineteenth century of sandstone quarried in the Forest of Dean, was never built for war, despite its striking resemblance to the thirteenth-century castles that Edward I had built to ward the Welsh borders.

Eventually, Cookie and Freddy declared an uneasy truce; both cats studiously ignoring each other or growling menacingly at thin air when the other came too close. Sometimes Freddy is unable to resist an opportunity to deliver a swift surprise blow at Cookie. In general, however, the cats have a pretty good life. They put on their separate performances in front of visitors – Cookie in the entrance hall, Freddy idly sprawled out in state in the Red Room. They take turns to visit the children's playroom, and feed in strict rotation.

Outside there is ample to keep the two adversaries distracted, although some of the curiosities and activities of this busy castle are more welcomed by the cats than others. Take for example, the steam traction engine that stands in the courtyard. For a lurking cat it's ideal – plenty of good smells, excellent cover, especially under a protective tarpaulin.

Picture Freddy, sauntering unaware through the gatehouse, meeting his perfectly reliable hiding place clanking slowly towards him snorting steam and hissing angrily. Cookie might have taken pleasure at Freddy's terrifying encounter, had she not long fled in terror from her vantage point in the entrance hall.

The castle's adventure playground, which should allow Cookie and Freddy to let off steam independently, has also become a source of discord. Cookie happened to stumble upon Freddy as he was slithering rather tentatively down the slide, and seized a rare chance to leap upon his back as he was dizzily regaining his feet.

They do declare a sort of truce when there are corporate activity days. The sight of panic-stricken executives, struggling to overcome imaginary hazards with rudimentary materials, is enough to distract the most aggressive cat. For a moment, both Freddy and Cookie stretch out idly in the branches overlooking these strange humans, marvelling at why they have to build a rope bridge to cross a perfectly good path.

A deceptively benign Freddy, fresh from the fray

Sumo

Sumo is adorned with a name that is entirely fitting.
For he is large and will grapple with anybody:
dogs, goats and human beings.

Even Sumo just can't open that gate

An early morning stroll
through the maze

Sumo's *pièce de résistance* entails leaping onto the shoulders of the unwary passer-by. His owner recalls walking, one pitch-black and stormy winter night, past the churchyard from his local pub, the Henry VIII. When he heard a spectral rustling in the undergrowth, he apprehensively increased his pace. But, to his dismay, so did the rustling.

As he approached the bridge there was a maniacal scrabble and, as Doug broke into a frantic dash for home, a beaming Sumo flew through the air, landing with a purring thump on his shoulders. There is no malice in Sumo – the wrestling started as kitten play and, well, he just got bigger.

This jovial colossus of a cat has the good fortune to live with Doug Goodyer, the Head Gardener at Hever Castle, where he has the run of thirty-five acres of formal and informal garden, an enormous lake, a castle whose foundations date back to the twelfth century, as well as a Tudor village reconstructed by the Astor family, a garden shop and restaurants.

With such a large territory in which to keep himself exercised – and all the sparring – one would expect Sumo to be a little more streamlined. Many, however, are the sources of nourishment. He regularly rolls home every night at seven o'clock for large meals. He is never fooled when the clocks go either forward or backward. Furthermore, there are the treats that come from the Estate Office and, best of all, the rich pickings from visitors to the Moat and Pavilion restaurants, set in the castle grounds. Doug confesses he doesn't understand how such an enormous and obviously well-fed cat convinces people that he is ravenous. But Sumo is a consummate actor and must rehearse his forlorn expressions in the bathroom mirror.

A castle cat at complete ease

It's no wonder that Doug feared a ghost when Sumo stalked him through the undergrowth. The castle history during the time of Henry VIII was unhappy. The king cultivated an unwelcome passion for Anne Bullen (later known as Boleyn), whose family lived at Hever during the fifteenth century. He made frequent and unwanted visits to Hever and became determined to marry her and – he hoped – to father the male heir he so desperately desired. The refusal of the Church to dissolve his previous marriage to Catherine of Aragon resulted in the creation of the Church of England, the English Reformation and the Dissolution of the monasteries.

Sumo enforces the castle regulations

Poor childless Anne was eventually executed at the Tower of London. The fortunes of the rest of the Bullen family declined rapidly too, with the deaths of Anne's mother and father, and execution of her brother Lord Rochford. Henry then appropriated Hever Castle, and gave it to the equally hapless Anne of Cleves. No one told me that there were ghosts but if there were, they might well be those of the luckless Bullen family.

Sumo lives his life oblivious to all this. He loves the castle. The moat water has a certain vintage bouquet and he regularly waits by the portcullis to join the tours. He shows particular interest in an eighteenth-century tapestry depicting a hunting scene which hangs above the Inner Hall. The torture implements kept in the Council Chamber also fascinate him, and perhaps he thinks that no torturer, however devious, would have got the better of him.

A drinker of vintage moat water

Curiously, although he adores people, Sumo is not a homebody. True, he keeps his dinner date every night, and the dogs sigh in resignation as he breezes in, for they know that the after-dinner entertainment is always a series of short wrestling bouts that they never win. After dusting down the dogs and banging noses with them to show there are no hard feelings, Sumo, who studiously ignores the other three family cats (Pluto, Chester and Mars), paces around before once more heading out on his nightly rounds.

He eventually retires to a nest with Tracy and Sharon the goats, selected for their combat skills and, more practically, for the comfort of their angora wool. In summer the garden shop keeps a cushioned box, from which he can keep a sleepy eye on the caterer's deliveries and the number of visitors making for the restaurants. Sumo is fully in sympathy with the legacy of lavishness bequeathed by the Astor family, which took over the castle in the early 1900s. A cat that lives on a diet of tea, pilchards, moat water and the special-of-the-day at the restaurant has no need of supplementary hunting. The ducks and other waterfowl that populate the lake and moat don't even bother to look up when Sumo is about.

Ghadafi

Ghadafi has a recurring problem: he can't make up
his mind whether he is a castle cat or a pub cat.

Ghadafi invites a favourable comparison

Peter Frost was working as a vet in Broughton, a small town in the Lake District, not far from Muncaster Castle, when a farmer came in with a cat that was having difficulty giving birth. Peter delivered the litter, three perfect tabbies and one coal black male. The black kitten was the last one out, and Peter claimed it for his own. However, when Peter lifted up the mother to check that she was all right the kitten, still attached by the birth cord, was also hoisted into the air dangling in astonishment in front of his prospective owner!

The kitten was named Vic and took up residence with Peter in his flat above the veterinary surgery. It wasn't long before Peter realized that Vic, far from being a tranquil little companion, was actually a tyrant in thin disguise. As a young male cat, he nearly dismembered a dog belonging to one of the surgery nurses – a dog doing nothing except snoozing under a table. To reflect international events at the time, Vic became Ghadafi.

Peter had already adopted an overweight springer spaniel called Britt. She quickly rued the fact that she had long ears, because Ghadafi decided that they were just the right size to hang from. He was frequently told off for his bad behaviour and – on one occasion – walked out, taking up residence in a local pub, the Manor Arms. His hideaway was eventually discovered, and Ghadafi returned home to find that Peter, who had recently married, was making plans to move to Muncaster Castle, the family home of his wife, Iona.

Wondering whether he dare escape to the local pub

The visitor to Muncaster is confronted by a wooden carving of a wildcat in the outer hall of the castle. This is the family emblem and Ghadafi is rather proud of it. He seems to steer visitors towards anything that bears the emblem, and will leap ahead to stand by the wildcat, inviting a favourable comparison. People remark at the heraldic ferocity of the emblem, then call Ghadafi a 'cute kitty'. As we know, he is definitely not a cute kitty.

He restores his pride by creeping into the owl sanctuary. He slinks round to the enclosure of a really ferocious eagle owl, waits until he thinks the owl isn't looking and then growls through the safety wire.

One day, pretending to follow the Frost-Penningtons on a long walk, Ghadafi scooted off into a convivial looking pub. He assumed no one knew his background, and he could pretend to be abandoned and under-fed. However he hadn't bothered to read the pub sign. It was the Pennington Arms, hardly a guarantee of anonymity for a Pennington cat.

Ghadafi recovers from an encounter with an eagle owl

How could anyone call Ghadafi a 'cute kitty'!

Blackie

Blackie gives every impression of being a grizzled
retainer and one wonders whether he has been
at the castle since it was acquired by
Thomas de Ingilby in the twelfth century.

Blackie starts his boundary patrol

He sports dreadlocks, suggesting that grooming isn't high among his daily list of priorities. Frequently scarred, he also costs a small fortune in veterinary bills, but is evidently indestructible.

The truth is that Blackie is as close to being a wild cat living in a castle as it is possible to be. Colin Claydon, the castle caretaker, looks after him and believes he is about fifteen years old, although no one knows for sure. He was probably abandoned by someone who left the village and, as any sensible estate dweller would do, he turned to the Ingilbys for succour.

His centre of operations is in the old furnace room — what a blessing the heating boilers are for castle cats. His daily routine is as regular as clockwork, starting with a nine o'clock breakfast provided by Colin Claydon, followed by the ritual placement of muddy footprints on the cars of Sir Thomas and Lady Ingilby. Rodent catching is his forte, and mindful of the debt of care he owes the castle, he pursues this with ruthless vigour.

He patrols the castle boundaries, and woe betide the village cats foolish enough to think that they might just potter along to see what's happening at the castle. Their sorties are abruptly halted by a furious Blackie, who knows all the lookout points and ambush sites. His scars bear witness to many defensive battles.

I firmly believe that cats sense atmosphere and maybe Blackie has inherited the spirit of Jane Ingilby — a prodigious fighter known as 'Trooper Ingilby'. The Ingilbys were a staunch Royalist family, and after the rout of Royalist forces at the battle of Marston Moor, an exhausted Cromwell decided to camp his troops at Ripley whilst he stayed the night in the castle. It was left to Trooper Jane to entertain Cromwell, which she did, by refusing him food or bed, spending the evening pointing two pistols at his head. She had cause to regret not discharging the pistols though, as a vengeful Cromwell had his Royalist prisoners executed by the gatehouse the following morning: the marks of the musket balls can still be seen.

Blackie's ferocious loyalty hasn't brought such dire consequences, and he is free to enjoy not only the extensive estate, with lakes and a deer park, but the glasshouses in the walled garden containing the Hull University botanical collection and the herbaceous borders. He's particularly fond of hyacinths.

He likes a good defensive position

Brandy

Rockingham withstood six full years of siege,
but a succession of cats have managed to find
their way in.

A well-read castle cat

The castle was built on the orders of William the Conqueror in the eleventh century, occupying a site used by the Saxons as a defensive position against marauding Vikings. Protected on three sides by steep slopes and ravines, a massive curtain wall guards the remainder of the site. It's not surprising that Rockingham withstood that siege by the forces of Henry III, and only fell to the Parliamentarians in the Civil War because they used siege cannon.

Admittedly the first Rockingham cat – Tiger – gained entrance to the castle by dishonourable means. He is thought to have been smuggled on the school bus by David, one of the Saunders Watson children, and placed quietly within the castle grounds. Perhaps with his brothers and sisters as conspirators, David feigned surprise at finding the cat there.

Tiger ignored a former cook's warning: 'No person whether belonging to the family or not is ever, under any pretext, to enter the kitchen without first obtaining leave.'

Cats know that rules are only for humans and dogs, and he made his home in the old Victorian kitchen. Alas, the kitchen was no longer a scene of bustling food preparation; the great spit remained bare and Tiger had to be content with dreams of what could have been if only he had lived a hundred years ago. He might have met his match in such a daunting cook and ended up haunting the Street – a group of buildings with a game larder, dairy, brew house and bakery attached to the curtain wall: not such a bad place in its heyday for a cat. After three years Tiger disappeared, and down from the stables came an unwanted black-and-white kitten.

Brandy: the castle kitchen is her favourite haunt

Carlos was discovered, frantically trying to shove large amounts of white feathers under the yew hedge. He was banished in disgrace, thankful only that the portcullis didn't descend on him as he fled.

Whatever edict was issued barring cats from the castle didn't reach as far as the stables and, before long, a wobbly little kitten made her way through the gatehouse. Her unsteady gait (which may well have earned her the name Brandy) and two syllable miaow – which sounds uncannily like 'hello' – gained her reluctant admission.

The resident cocker spaniels accepted this new arrival with benign disinterest as she also took up residence in the kitchen. Once she had appreciated the delicacy of her situation, however, she set about finding somewhere unobtrusive to spend her nights. A spacious vaulted subterranean boiler room serves Brandy well. Not only does it provide warm sleeping quarters but it is also the starting point for several private tunnels carrying heating pipes into various parts of the castle.

Brandy's tastes are fairly typical of a castle cat. Roast pheasant is a particular favourite, but she is not a born thief. Rather than making a decisive getaway, she hides in the pantry. She should thank her lucky stars that it is Mrs Saunders Watson who reproves her. Maybe Brandy's cautious nature can be attributed to nocturnal encounters with the ghost of King John – first summoned up during a seance in which he let it be known that he had not lost his treasure in the infamous crossing of the Wash but buried it at Rockingham. If the ghost of King John isn't enough for Brandy, there's a headless warrior who rides through the gatehouse and the ghost that Charles Dickens saw during his stay.

Brandy makes a break for the infamous elephant hedge

Carlos, as he was promptly named, had no inhibitions about where he would go, and made straight for the kitchen – this time the one the family uses. Carlos showed strong interest in the white doves that lived in the castle dovecote. These have a small place in the castle's history, as Charles Dickens referred to them in his novel *Bleak House*, partly written at Rockingham.

Commander Saunders Watson had been puzzled and concerned by the dwindling numbers of doves until

Smudge, Marley and Bumble

A curio of this almost-island off the south coast
of Cornwall is the castle's mummified cat.
It came back from Egypt with the second Lord
St Levan to whom it had seemed an interesting find
during his travels in the Middle East.

Smudge checks his secret entrance

The Mount itself was supposedly built by a giant — Cormoran — who regularly waded ashore to take a few cattle. This legend gave rise to a story beloved of generations of children, *Jack the Giant Killer*.

When the Tophams first arrived at St Michael's Mount, their four cats — Smudge, Pod, Marley and Bumble — gaped in horror, but not at the giant. They were used to boats and water, having lived in coastal towns and villages before. However they were not going to allow themselves to be placed in a thing that looked like a cross between a tank and a trawler. This is the amphibious vehicle that crosses the flooded causeway to the island. The cats were unceremoniously hoisted aboard.

The next morning brought even more ominous signs. When the cats stuck their heads out of the window, they were startled to see a row of extremely large and malevolent herring gulls staring back at them. There was no escape. They could not read the tide tables and there was an awful lot of exposed territory between them and the mainland: they had observed the gulls dive-bombing some unfortunate fish.

A quick wash and brush up before the tour arrives

Smudge keeps a wary watch on the herring gulls

A gravestone provides good camouflage for Marley

They decided to stay and it fell to Bumble to make the first outside sortie. Two dogs put him off his guard and his familiarization exercise turned into a spell of living wild on the island. He reappeared six weeks later, thin, but unbowed. Now he keeps very close to the Tophams' cottage and frantically stocks up on the other cats' food, just in case he has to take another enforced leave of absence.

Pod, described as the ugliest cat in Christendom and named after his likeness to certain creatures in a space drama, died shortly after moving to the island. He is buried in a peaceful overgrown pets' graveyard on the hillside under the castle wall. Marley – like his namesake Bob Marley, the renowned reggae singer – is a pretty laid-back cat.

Meanwhile Smudge sets out each morning, braving gulls and dogs to welcome visitors to the island, with its history that spans from the fourth century BC to the present day – a fascinating mixture of sea trade, monasticism, pilgrimage, legend, siege, rebellion and, latterly, relative domestic calm. Smudge enigmatically escorts them to the West Door of the castle, where they are welcomed and he is not. He has now found a way into the castle furnace room; he has befriended a member of staff who waits for him at the kitchen window. It can only be a matter of time before he masters the underground railway that carries stores from the bottom of the Mount to the castle.

A nervous Bumble makes an appearance

Marley waits for Smudge to let him out

William and Harriet

When suspected witches were burned at the
Tower of London their cats, condemned as 'familiars',
were walled up and left. One mummified specimen
was recently found in the White Tower.

Time out at the Tower: Harriet plays dead

In fact, there's quite a tradition of cats at the Tower. Some of the Tower army regiments allow cats to parade 'on regimental strength' for their rodent-catching prowess. The most celebrated account concerns Henry, third Earl of Southampton, who was imprisoned in the Tower by Elizabeth I for his part in the Essex rebellion. His cat found her way to the Tower and climbed down a chimney to join him in confinement: a contemporary portrait shows the Earl with her and, judging by the ferocity of the cat's expression, it's clear that she had little patience with those who wished to mistreat her master.

Today's Tower cats live in less oppressive times and some of them are to be found in the Casemates, a secluded area built by the Duke of Wellington around 1840 to house concealed gun batteries within the Tower precincts. The Casemates displaced a disorderly shanty town of ladies of easy virtue, ale vendors, gamblers and assorted hangers-on.

Colonel Hamish Mackinlay, lately Deputy Governor of the Tower, and his wife Elspeth brought their cats, William and Harriet, here from Norfolk. Given his responsibilities for security at the time, Colonel Mackinlay had no wish to see the cats fleeing through Traitor's Gate, or setting off the alarms in the White Tower, repository of the Crown Jewels. He knew that even doors raised above ground height to avoid battering rams and fire would be no obstacle to determined cats. William and Harriet were confined to quarters. They took their revenge by rubbing off as much fur as possible on any item of dress uniform or formal wear they could find in the house.

*Harriet savours
a respite from
William's courtship*

*William wistfully
reflects on what
might have been*

On patrol in the Casemates

Through a closed window, William made the acquaintance of Cleo and Bella, two neighbouring lady cats whose hopes of nights on the castle tiles were raised by his suggestive posturing. Harriet looked disdainful as she had previous experience of William's unwanted attentions knowing that, thanks to the vet, all concerned would remain celibate.

Baggins, a kindly cat living with the previous Chief Yeoman Warder, took Harriet and William under his paw, and seemed to ensure that they were fully briefed as to where they could go. He introduced them to the Casemates and spent many patient hours there trying to show them how to catch London pigeons. He warned against some larger birds – the Tower ravens – which, he pointed out, would have the cats' tails off in the shake of a whisker. That may be why the cats enjoy it when they drive back to the Mackinlays' Norfolk house. The pheasants there offer the cats the chance to be the pursuers and not the pursued.

Rosie

Sylvia Stephens regularly hears comments about
how royal her cat looks, and has several times
been asked whether Rosie belongs to the Queen.

Waiting to waylay visitors

It is certainly something to lay claim to being a castle cat at Windsor, which has belonged to the sovereigns of England for over 900 years and which is now one of the homes of Her Majesty Queen Elizabeth II.

Rosie's origins are humble, however. She comes from Liverpool where she had been rescued by Sylvia's son and daughter-in-law, Simon and Karen, who run an informal haven for lost and sick cats. When Mrs Stephens was first appointed as Domestic Bursar to St George's Chapel it was doubtful whether Rosie would be admitted to such an exclusive enclave. Animals were not encouraged but the chapter clerk kindly allowed that a pet already owned would be permitted resident's rights.

As the castle is possibly the largest fortress in the world, and in some respects like a fortified town, Rosie has sensibly decided to restrict her territory to the area of the castle where her owner lives. It encompasses St George's Chapel, St George's House and associated cloisters – all of which still represents a larger area than any other castle in the British Isles.

Other cats were in residence and a series of bitter battles with two canons' cats resulted in an uneasy truce. One of her opponents, a gentle ecclesiastical cat, has given up completely preferring the peace of Windsor Great Park. The other just won't learn, however, and to this day the Horseshoe Cloisters echo to some very unregal scenes of battle.

Rosie's other distraction is the wainscotting in her apartment. She sits with the patience of Job, waiting for some unsuspecting castle mouse to show its nose. If her own mice won't play, Rosie zips off to the sacristan's apartment, where the mice still haven't learned.

Still waiting for visitors

It was definitely not one of Rosie's better days

A frustrated Rosie warms herself on the office typewriter

She is a personable animal, although her human friendships show certain signs of cupboard love. A good friend, for example, is the Chapel heating engineer. She parades for the tourists in some of the most famous places: the Galilee Porch and the Pitkin Table, from which souvenirs are sold. She didn't appreciate the public relations potential of one of my visits, however, as she skulked moodily under bushes whenever I produced a camera.

The Chapel stewards show a benevolent tolerance towards Rosie to the extent of having a 'Rosie brush' handy to keep themselves spick and span. The process is known as a Royal brushoff. Rosie is a regular attendee at events where the Chapel and the Royal Household combine, but she never dares to venture inside the Chapel. She can often be seen casting a critical eye over the robes of the Garter Knights as they walk past. She personally knows a number of the military knights too and is usually there to twitch her tail at them as they process into the Chapel each Sunday.

Ginger

Lord help any dog, however large, unwise enough
to walk into the weaver's shed at Bunratty Castle.
Ginger springs from her basket under the loom,
ready for the fray, a raging if somewhat undersized
tigress. She'll put anything canine – up to
wolfhound size – to flight.

Twelve years ago Ginger, starving, ill and maltreated, turned to Bunratty Castle and its Folk Park for refuge. She made straight for the weaver's shed, where Yvonne Acheson was demonstrating her craft. How cats can sense a human of goodwill no one knows, but their judgements of people are usually unerring. Yvonne and her partner, Kay Bowman, took Ginger in and fed and cared for her until she was fit enough to brave her new surroundings. Ginger resolved to live her new life in the spirit of the old Irish saying – 'Ar scáth a chéile a mhaireas na daoine' (people live in one another's shelter).

Bunratty Castle is a fine example of a tower house built in the mid-fifteenth century by the O'Briens who, together with the McNamaras, had been assaulting, destroying and plundering previous castles on this site since it had been granted by Henry I to the de Clares. For a while there was peace, until the Civil War in England spread to Ireland and once again Bunratty was caught up in conflict.

The castle gradually declined until it was bought, derelict and ruined, by Lord Gort, who was responsible for its restoration. Today it has been restored again in period style, adjacent to an intriguing collection of reconstructed nineteenth-century Irish homes, the Folk Park – farmhouses, a fisherman's house, village streets, from the poorest to the grandest.

Once she was fit enough, Ginger prowled the castle and village, each new discovery confirming that she had ended up in a cat's paradise. She established a firm friendship with the castle custodian, John Collins, despite the fact that – like other castle cats – she was forever setting off the alarms. She explored the maze of rooms and staircases, and mercilessly expelled several stray cats whom fate, with a little assistance from

Off to see the 'women of the house'

A warm hearth and welcoming bed - Ginger is spoilt for choice

Ginger, had decreed were not to live at Bunratty.

Not being allowed to stay in the weaver's shed at night, she picked three gratifying alternatives – all with heating, of course. The first, a simple fisherman's house – Teach Iascaire Chaisín – has a good firm bed. Next to that is the blacksmith's forge – not quite so comfortable, but with a very good fire. Third, and by far the most fulfilling is the Teach na Míntíre – the Golden Vale Farmhouse. Ginger was passing here one day when an aroma akin to manna stopped her in her tracks. She put on a shameless display of pathos to gain entry and then briskly introduced herself to Ethna and Muriel, the 'Women of the House', who were responsible for this mouth-watering smell of home-baking.

Half an hour later, Ginger, stuffed to the whiskers with home-baked, milk-soaked bread and scones, staggered out of the kitchen door. She managed to weave her way to a ground floor bedroom, where she collapsed in a stupor of gluttony. Not surprisingly, this is now an important stop on Ginger's daily itinerary, not

Ruffled by the Shannon winds

least because she can sleep off her excesses overnight in the guest bedroom. And since there's nothing like freshly churned butter to accompany good baking, the dairy also gets an occasional visit.

In the castle, on a panel inset into a fourteenth-century Dower cupboard, a touching relief carving shows the Last Supper. Ginger is intrigued by the figure of a cat, sitting attentively under the table. This could be Ginger in rather more secular surroundings, as a regular guest at the evening banquets. Mounting another unabashed display of pretend malnourishment, she discreetly drags spare ribs out of the Great Hall. She lounges in the North Solar, nibbling away nonchalantly whilst idly glancing through the murder hole for any stray cat foolish enough to venture onto the drawbridge. If one comes, Ginger despatches a warning cascade of rib bones down onto the head of the bemused invader. Ginger must have succumbed to the charms of some visiting cats, for she has produced two fine litters of kittens. Two of her sons live with Yvonne in nearby Limerick.

Jupiter, Venus, Black Kidders and Lucky

The comings and goings of the Charleville Forest
Castle cats would be the envy of a well-organized
and busy railway station. Trying to disentangle
their genealogy is another matter.

Venus: ever alert to the castle spirits

No door keeps out a Charleville Forest castle cat

Black Kidders prefers a pre-emptive strike on Lucky

This large feline tribe prowls and glides through the fairy-tale castle of Charleville Forest. It was built by the great Irish architect Francis Johnston, and is considered to be a true Gothic masterpiece. Its position, shrouded by forest with turrets floating mysteriously above the trees, is enough to tantalize the dullest of imaginations. Constance Heavey-Alagna and her daughter, Bridget Vance, have been restoring this extraordinary place for the last six years. The scale of their undertaking is extraordinary, given the extent of damage caused by past vandalism and neglect.

The family was drawn back to Charleville through ancestral connections: the maternal family came from a simple stone cottage close by, and the great-grandparents had been imprisoned at one time by the original owners. The place clearly has a powerful atmosphere and, if humans can sense it, one can be sure that cats will too. And so to Charleville they came, singly and in pairs.

Molly (now deceased) was the first. A ghostly white Persian who haunted the surrounding woods courted her and in due course she gave birth to a litter that included two pure white kittens, Venus and Jasper. Venus was courted by her father. Of her kittens Jupiter (also pure white), twin tabbies Atun and Ashia, and their sister Alex survive.

A feline cold shoulder: Jupiter and Black Kidders

Even Constance's husband, who had given stern lectures on the follies of having so many cats, succumbed to the castle's spells, for the very next day he came back with a black-and-white kitten he had rescued and Venus generously adopted. The most recent cat, Black Kidders, arrived *in utero* when a visiting friend brought her pregnant cat to the castle. The kittens obligingly emerged but even Constance and Bridget felt they had to draw the line somewhere. Black Kidders was the one who was allowed to stay. To continue the lineage would take as much space as the book of Kings in the Old Testament. Suffice it to say that the castle is garrisoned by cats.

And as if they weren't enough, Constance decided that she needed a dog — Tigger — for company when she stayed at the old family cottage. Then Wolfie, a half-starved and maltreated border collie, showed up at the castle door. Lucky the cat nursed him unrelentingly, cleaning up his cuts and making him feel part of the family. This menagerie *à neuf* sleeps in a jumbled furry heap by the stove, tumbling around with Bridget's three children, Kate, Michael and Constance, and playing a death defying version of dog and cat tag through the outer ruins and gardens. The castle rats and mice have long since packed their bags — a rodent exodus of epic proportions!

Venus and Jupiter: part of the castle fabric

The main part of the restorations to date are the hall and entrance staircase, the gallery, drawing room, dining room and library. Underneath, and to the chapel side of the castle are the old butlers' quarters, warm and cosy, which serve as the daytime living area. The animals are theoretically restricted to this part of the castle, but in practice things are a little different. The cats know every nook and cranny from the whispering ruined rooms at the top, down the brooding, richly panelled – and hazardous – backstairs, through the lower restorations. In common with Constance and Bridget, they know the secret door that communicates with the old chapel. They are thoroughly familiar with every tunnel, opening and secret passage that penetrates the castle and its outbuildings.

I'm sure that they are aware of the ghosts too, and no one could convince me that this place doesn't have its share of unearthly, midnight occupants. Maybe the animals communicate with their own kind, for there is both a cats' cemetery and two eighteenth-century dogs' tombs in the grounds. As for the spectral child who escorted one of Bridget's children out of danger, the cats of Charleville leave that to the reader's imagination.

Bowes, Chester and Kittie

When Brian Thompson moved to Cloghan,
he made the journey in the company of three cats,
three dogs, a lamb and a hedgehog.

Crenellation-hopping: Kittie's favourite sport

They had theretofore lived a convivial life together at Emmel Castle. Kittie, Bowes and Chester, the three cats, liked nothing better than to stroll down the drive in the company of the other animals, including the rather breathless hedgehog.

Brian's wife Elyse suggested the family estate car. That way the animals could keep each other's spirits up – fine in theory, but disastrous in practice. Chester and Harry the Hedgehog huddled together in terror on the back of Elyse's seat. Bowes lay on the dashboard seeming to urge Brian that he had made a big mistake, whilst Kittie decided that she would leave substantial signs of her protest all over the car. The lamb just bleated plaintively all the way. And the shame of it all was that the Thompsons had gone to endless trouble to make a great welcome at Cloghan Castle.

A thirty-foot Christmas tree stood in the seventeenth-century Great Hall. A welcoming fire blazed at one end, and brimming bowls of food were set out in the kitchen. Bowes was having none of it. She sprang up into the Christmas tree – startling wildlife, which had been slow to realize that their home was on the move – and remained there throughout the festival. It was an unusual tree, topped by a glaring and decidedly unfestive cat.

Kittie and Chester then proceeded to disappear every day – leaving after breakfast and returning in time for dinner, their whereabouts a mystery until a puzzled neighbouring farmer recounted how they'd been catching rats in return for a taste or two of the cream off the milk.

Bowes likes a quiet read

Bowes: an above stairs cat

Back in the fold, Bowes was distracted by the arrival of puppies, whom she mothered with great affection. Kittie and Chester devised a novel form of exercise – crenellation-hopping along the bawn wall. Chester now takes this to extremes, climbing out of a tower window, along a roof ridge, and up a sheer wall to the Thompson's bedroom window, where he waits for them to fall asleep before letting rip with a cadenza of heart-rending and completely fake shrieks. Meanwhile the cats look on as Brian Thompson winches up 150 loads of stones to the top of the keep to rebuild the battlements.

Cloghan has a chequered history. It's curious that it was Brian Thompson who saw the spectre of a wild warrior rather than the cats who are always sensitive to the supernatural. The castle was adapted from a monastery by the Normans who were then expelled by the 'Great O'Madden'. His family lived at Cloghan for

Chester is a professional snoozer

some 250 years before being bloodily ousted by the English, who threw forty-six people off the battlements to their death. (Some skeletons have been unearthed below that spot.) Twice more the castle changed hands, lost to the Cromwellians in 1651, and taken from the Jacobites by the Williamites in 1691. The reason for the military significance of such a comparatively small castle was its position, dominating one of the few safe crossing places on the river Shannon.

Visitors to Cloghan are shown a ceramic model of the castle prior to their tour. Suddenly a smug Kittie emerges from inside, certain in the knowledge that she has completely wrecked the introductory talk. She then climbs on to Elyse's shoulders for the rest of the tour. All the cats enjoy making mischief when visitors are around, slinking into positions guaranteed to distract the most earnest student of Irish history.

Polo, FatCat, Sphinx
and the Farm Cats

Like his owner, Karen Sykes, Farm Cat One
is never happier than when he is on the back
of a pony.

Farm Cat One gets ready for lift-off

Sphinx: the warden of the keep

The inscrutable Sphinx

He has devised an unusual system for propelling himself at high speed towards unsuspecting birds who, frankly, do not expect to be attacked by a mounted cat. The cat and pony approach a suitable target. The cat sinks his claws into the pony's back. The resulting and spectacular convulsion launches the cat towards his intended victim at great speed. Many a bird breathes a sigh of relief as a badly aimed and flailing cat rockets by.

Springfield Castle is truly the domain of cats, for only they can easily slip in through the thickets of brambles that guard its entrances. From the lofty keep, they observe the coming and going of visitors and keep an eye on the general goings-on around the farm.

Home of the Fitsgeralds of Claonghlais, and latterly the Muskerrys, there has been a castle here since the twelfth century. The ruined Desmond Keep stands as a romantic backdrop to the family house (Georgian, but rebuilt using the original walls after it burnt down in 1921 during the Irish Civil War). Springfield Castle also enjoys the distinction of having been a haven for Irish culture frequented by musicians and Bardic Poets. The bustle of life at the castle was written about by one of Ireland's greatest seventeenth-century poets, Dáibhí Ó Bruadair.

These days the castle is home to a thriving deer farm and visitor centre, while ten-year-old Karen Sykes ministers to the needs of a demanding group of cats, some of whom she has subtly introduced. Two Abyssinian cats were the first official cats of Springfield, one of whom gave birth to two litters from which two kittens were retained – FatCat and Sphinx.

Not content with the cats that she had, Karen purchased two needy kittens from a local fair. The house

Quality assurance: FatCat and Sphinx prepare for guests

Polo's nerves are steadied by FatCat

was already bulging with cats, hamsters, gerbils and tadpoles, and when they were old enough, Karen's parents, Jonathan and Betty Sykes, installed the kittens at the farm where they could earn their keep by rodent catching. A warm hayloft provides shelter and they have their riding ponies and deer to keep them company.

Karen then tested her parents' serenity by acquiring yet another kitten. Sensing an impending crisis, Tanzania, one of the Abyssinian cats who had just had her own litter of kittens, whisked the new kitten – a little white thing called Polo – together with her own litter, out of the house and up into the fork of a nearby tree. When the time came for the kittens to leave their tree home, Polo had grown so fat that he was wedged in position. Only a ladder and human intervention could dislodge him.

The cats wander at will among the red and fallow deer, an appealing sight on the face of it unless one knows that the cats might just be inspecting their dinner 'on the hoof'. They also get to go on holiday, accompanying the Sykes to their beach cottage, and diving headfirst into bowls of fresh prawns. The extraordinary Sphinx dives into the sea, swimming with the children to a small offshore island.

Sheba

Nearly drowned on a Cambridgeshire farm,
Sheba now lives in one of the largest inhabited
castles in Ireland.

Tullynally's multitude of rooms give Sheba plenty of scope for choice

Snow is best appreciated from the inside!

She is living testimony to cats' changing fortunes, or perhaps to their fabled nine lives. The Pakenhams' son, Ned, made an eleventh-hour rescue bid for her whilst staying on a farm in England. He took her back to Bristol where he was at university, and installed her in his flat. He then had to restructure a hectic university social life in order to care for, and clean up after this tiny mute kitten.

She couldn't be separated from her Samaritan and would scatter his papers over the floor and tear pages out of library books as he worked. She accompanied him to various social events, the sight of her inquisitive head emerging from the depths of his jacket in the student bar becoming quite a conversation piece. So it was with mixed feelings, during a visit to the family's London home (with Sheba in tow), that he concurred

Gardening intrigues Sheba

with his mother Valerie's suggestion to despatch Sheba to Tullynally. On the quiet he was captivated by this silent little cat.

Sheba treated her arrival there with the same regal indifference as her namesake, accepting that her new home should be a sprawl of turrets, towers and battlements covering over two acres of ground. Exploring a castle with 120 rooms takes some doing and, when you don't have a voice, you need to be sure of your lines of retreat. One day Sheba was inadvertently locked in a bathroom, where she remained for a week. A dripping tap saved her life and she seemed no less confident thereafter. Her predecessor, Loretta, insisted on being taken back to London.

Sheba keeps a low public profile, disdainfully ignoring the dogs that live around the courtyard but doggedly following Valerie Pakenham when she is tending the gardens in the evening. It is a different matter when the

Sheba sets off to visit her doting feline admirers at the farm

family gathers in the castle. Sheba takes pride of place, joining the family for meals and taking particular interest in the regular concerts in the Great Hall. She has definite musical opinions. Chamber music commands her entire attention, and she gazes intently as the musicians draw their bows across violin, viola and cello strings. She has even been known to pluck at a cello string or two. The action of the hammers in the grand piano also intrigues her, although she has discovered she can't depress the notes and watch the mechanical action at the same time.

Despite her own dexterity at the keyboard, Sheba is terrified by the organ in the Great Hall. The breathy quality of an eight-foot flute pipe makes her leap for cover. She enjoyed a Van Morrison rock recital, but was perplexed at the great man's insistence on humble boiled chicken and decaffeinated coffee. She expected rock musicians to have rather more exotic tastes. There's jazz too, when Sheba can really be a cool cat, tripping across the snare drum.

Tigger MacCat and Shelley

Shelley was at a disadvantage when marmalade
upstart Tigger MacCat needed chasing off his patch
– he only has three legs.

Tigger MacCat: always checking the gardeners

Tigger's arrival needs explaining. She had given birth to a litter of four kittens in the sawmill adjacent to Brodick Castle. She was in a remote corner of the yard, well concealed behind a stack of timber until someone decided to move it. Much to her irritation, Tigger and her litter were exposed both to the gaze of the outside world and the noise of the sawmill, against which the timber had acted as a sound baffle.

After a tiresome week, Tigger MacCat had had enough. She packed up, hauled her kittens over the wall, and found herself in the nursery of Brodick Castle gardens. A new and much improved home was improvised in a bale of straw, where she was eventually discovered by the Head Gardener, Nigel Price. Fortunately, he did everything to accommodate Tigger MacCat and her family. The kittens were found homes, a flap was cut into the potting shed in case of extreme island winter weather, and Nigel's daughter Abigail, herself a cat owner, took up feeding duties.

Tigger MacCat was delighted with her new surroundings, and as soon as her censorious audience of young ones was safely housed elsewhere and she had the place to herself, Tigger MacCat resumed the serious business of lying on her back waggling legs in the air, leaping at gardeners' legs and chasing shadows.

With time on her hands, she also set out to explore her new home. She needed plenty of time too, for Brodick Castle, with its gardens and country park, is vast. The full potential of the gardens was realized by the Duchess of Montrose in the 1920s, who started the woodland garden with a gift of rhododendrons from Muncaster Castle. This garden has been developed and extended to become a horticultural treasure house.

The history of Brodick extends far back in time to

Still trying to spot the gardeners

when the Vikings used the site for defensive reasons. The earliest traceable part of the castle dates from the thirteenth century. A baronial tower was added in the late sixteenth century, and Cromwellian troops constructed a battery about seventy years later.

Luckily all the gardeners took to Tigger MacCat, including the propagator, Clare Reaney, who arrived later with her own two cats, Katie and Shelley. Clare took the precaution of keeping them indoors for a while, partly because it was winter and partly to 'home' them. Shelley spent the time glued to the window overlooking the nursery. The plants didn't interest him, neither did the pleasant outlook. Why, he wanted to know, was there a small marmalade cat strolling through his patch. And how could this human, Clare Reaney, be so insensitive to play with this other cat – right in front of Shelley too.

Tigger MacCat spotted Shelley, and brazenly flaunted her freedom, despite the enormous grounds of Brodick Castle open to her. Before too long, the two cats were scrutinizing one another, nose to nose through the glass. Shelley almost burst with frustration: there was no way he was going to have this little marmalade upstart taking centre stage.

Finally the day came for his release. Shelley crouched at the door, as though he was on starting blocks. The door was opened, and off he went – not like a bullet from a gun, but with a lurching tripedal wobble. Clearly, ambush would be the only way. He contrived a series of surprise attacks from underneath shrubs and behind walls, catching Tigger MacCat several times.

Tigger in turn realized that the advantage lay in height. When it comes to scrambling up steep banks, streaking up trees and clambering over rocks, Shelley is 'altitudinally disadvantaged'. Tigger MacCat just sits up a tree, watching Shelley hop around in frustration.

Early morning nursery games

Shelley — a three-legged tabby with a fine turn of speed

Moses and Zoe

Iain Crisp thinks that Moses is still a street-wise West London cat, a real 'chancer'. He is one of the castle cats of Crathes, numerous enough to form their own clan.

Zoe watches Moses with disdain

Moses I understood to be the castle garden cat. Then I heard of Zoe, who lives in the castle itself, whilst at Kennel Cottage – where the old castle kennels used to be – live Fionn, Liath and Froachie, whose gaelic names translate respectively to 'White', 'Grey' and 'Heather'. 'Beastie' is believed to be the name of the other regular cat, who appears frequently in the summer.

Marigold and William Bowman recently arrived to administrate Crathes Castle on behalf of the National Trust for Scotland, bringing Zoe the cat with them. The castle is the home of the Horn of Leys, given to Alexander Burnard by Robert the Bruce as a token of rights to the Royal Hunting Forest of Drum. The Bowmans had a sense that Crathes was good for cats as during a previous visit Marigold had met Moses drinking nonchalantly from a fountain. She was particularly taken with his relaxed attitude to being photographed – an attitude I wished had been shared by the Castle Fraser cats.

Moses belongs to Iain Crisp, the First Gardener at Crathes, and his family. He spends nearly all his time breezing around the castle grounds and gardens. He calls in at home for a regular feed but, with six children in waiting, he is quickly off out again. Trees and herbaceous

Moses keeps an eye on the garden from his stone bath

plants don't tweak his ears or try to dress him up in doll's clothes.

Despite his London provenance as the offspring of a rescued cat, and unlike Percy at Penhow, he has taken with gusto to the joys of garden life. Since the arrival of the Bowmans just before Christmas 1994, he has also investigated the castle with its new feline inhabitant. He usually enters by the pantry window.

Moses has earned his laurels by virtually eradicating the rats and rabbits that otherwise wreak havoc in the gardens. On cold winter nights he sneaks into bed with the Crisps' rather disinterested dog, judiciously waiting until the dog is asleep before joining him.

Seed propagators in the greenhouses sometimes serve as a hot-water bottle substitute, and recently, in a spell of bitterly cold weather, Moses persuaded William and Marigold Bowman that a discarded sweater in the castle porch would do very well.

The Bowmans' cat Zoe came from Cornwall, and is still quietly settling into castle life. She watches Moses disapprovingly from her window in the Bowmans' Queen Anne apartments as he potters round the garden. I rather suspect she thinks he's a bit of a ruffian. Zoe has her own way of keeping warm in the cold castle. She sticks to the beds, cleverly following the sun from room to room. The Bowmans have noticed that when

Moses can just squeeze through the arrow slits

she curls up into a tight ball, the weather invariably turns cold. She is supposed to stretch out more when the weather is due to improve, but in practice she forgets, leading to wrong predictions from the family.

Meanwhile Moses eats wherever he finds food, be it still or moving. Apparently he used to share the previous Head Gardener's sandwiches with him everyday, at twelve-thirty sharp. He specializes in entertaining visitors, and can usually be found escorting them round the fine herbaceous borders. If there is no one around he sits in an old stone bath, keeping a watchful eye out. If it is really quiet, he joins the rangers on their guided nature walks. Perhaps he's seeking to learn more about the habits of his prey. He definitely knows that where there are guided walks, there is usually a packed lunch or two.

Beastie, a shorthaired brindle cat, belongs to one of the foresters living on the estate and camps out in the laurel bushes during the summer. She quickly cottoned on to Moses' techniques. As the two cats battled in the rose beds, the rangers realized that while Moses was distracting one party, Beastie had been escorting the other, hence the fight.

Relations will probably improve. If either cat needs to take out its aggression, it can use a 140-foot high redwood tree for a scratching post.

George

The arms of Elizabeth, Countess of Sutherland, depict a rampant wildcat, the motto above which reads 'Sans peur'. A rather smaller cat, with a purr, roams the castle and estate of Dunrobin, ancient seat of the Sutherlands.

Good drains lie buried in the oldest part of Dunrobin

George likes to be liked

George belongs to Christopher Whealing and his wife Sarah. He started life with them in Cumbria, and got a rude shock when he was left with a friend, while they went off on a round-the-world cycling trip. George and his new custodian got on famously, to the extent that the Whealings had almost to resort to catnapping to get George back on their return. To add insult to injury for George, they acquired another cat – Nikki – and the whole family moved to Dunrobin Castle.

George and Nikki tolerated the journey with remark-able good humour, until they reached the Drumochter

Not every cat has a personal turret

Summit in a blizzard, whereupon George slumped, head in paws, wondering if there were any sane human beings left. If there were, they weren't making their way to the far north of Scotland. Their arrival was more auspicious. Christopher and Sarah were to live in the Factor's House within the policies of Dunrobin Castle. George discovered a small turret with outside steps, from where he could survey his new domain, a wide expanse of North Sea coast,

extensive woods, and a large, ornate castle, buried in the middle of which is the original tower of 1400.

George was continually frustrated in his attempts to colonize the bedrooms, and he and Nikki maintained an uneasy relationship. The dust was settling, and life was becoming bearable, when one morning George sauntered into the kitchen. He didn't get his usual warm welcome. In fact Sarah and Christopher were gazing into a padded box, from which strange gurgling

Bird watching from the library

noises were coming. With the arrival of a baby, it finally dawned on George that he had an unchallengeable rival. He stormed out.

As a good hunter, he had already ranged a fair distance, and now was spotted more and more frequently, morosely mooching along the distant beach (stopping long enough only for him to chase some unsuspecting seabird). A burn near the house prevented him seeking consolation in the town and so he travelled further and further into the woods. Even after his return, George continued his expeditions until one day he came across the castle.

Dunrobin Castle stands on a prominent bluff overlooking the Dornoch Firth. The original castle dates from the thirteenth century and, although completely encased by a Victorian architect in a 'Franco-Scots' palace, can still be seen as part of the central courtyard. George liked it. There were interesting drains, good odours. The entrance hall and main staircase were a different matter, as they could easily have accommodated his little stone turret, with room to spare for another one on top. George wasn't quite sure about the stags' heads on the wall which seemed to watch him as he scampered up, creeping with some relief into the drawing room before passing into the library, where he discovered a superb vantage point over the gardens to the seashore – a window sill offering endless opportunities for bird watching.

The difficulty about being a cat in an enormous castle is that having spotted one's bird, the subsequent dash down through the castle into the gardens – discounting the time used up when one skids round a corner to come face-to-face with a large and very aggressive looking suit of armour – takes long enough for one's intended victim to have died of old age. Large castles and hunting cats have to compromise, and George contents himself, for the most part, with Viking like sorties from the seashore. And, after all, he has a miniature castle tower of his own.

Ellie and Tigger

It is a strange situation when cats live in fear of birds.
But when you live on Skye, some of the birds are
big – bigger than dogs, in fact.

Ellie considers taking on the buzzards

These are big ugly things, with talons, that swoop silently out of the sky and don't go to the bird table. The buzzard, the golden eagle and the white-tailed sea eagle make regular passes over the cats' haunts, especially if it's around eleven in the morning, when they're feeling like a little snack to keep them going until lunch.

For Ellie and Tigger, castle cats of Dunvegan, nature on this 45,000 acres of estate is red in tooth and claw. Their rude awakening came when they were barked at by brown and great grey atlantic seals. Having recovered from seeing things that sounded like dogs, but lay on the ground and had funny legs, both cats took another closer look at Jenny the labrador.

The Dunvegan cats actually belong to Carrie and Laura Lambert, daughters of John Lambert – the MacLeod Estates Director – and his wife Sue. Carrie's first cat Angus, a great mouser with a propensity for falling off roofs, had died. Like all true cat lovers, Carrie found that life without a cat was incomplete. One day Sue Lambert returned from a shopping trip to Inverness, a major expedition entailing a brief ferryboat crossing and protracted drive over the mountains.

Carrie was asked to help unload the car and, as she started to lift the last container (covered for some reason by a coat), was startled to hear a protesting squeak from what she thought was a box of fruit! An indignant longhaired Persian kitten emerged to a rapturous welcome. She wasn't really indignant. It's just that Persians always look indignant. In fact, it was love at first sight.

Ellie isn't as innocent as she looks

Where's the banquet!

There was another welcome waiting inside for the kitten. Jenny the labrador was also pleased to see a new cat, an interest that Ellie discouraged with hisses which wouldn't disgrace a king cobra. Carrie's older sister Laura had her own preoccupation – horses; but such was Ellie's appeal, that her thoughts strayed towards having a cat of her own.

Another shopping trip to Inverness followed, with Laura and Carrie this time. And sure enough, on returning to the car, Laura found a chinchilla Persian kitten sitting on the front seat, trying to climb the seat belt. This new family addition, called Tigger, had a better view than Ellie on the return journey and stared with alarm as they crossed over to Skye. When he saw

Dunvegan Castle he was stupefied!

James Boswell, commenting to Lady MacLeod of Dunvegan Castle, said: 'It looks as if it had been let down from heaven by the four corners.' Certainly the castle's magnificent lochside setting does give it a fairy-like quality. It appears to be an integrated Victorian design, but within there are a series of much older buildings. These in their turn have been built on a site that was a fort a thousand years earlier. The oldest of the buildings is Leod's original fort, dating from the thirteenth century. This comprises a massive curtain wall to the seaward, pierced by a durus*, with portcullis and wooden barbican. The keep was added in the fourteenth century by the third Chief, Malcolm, and the

* Gaelic for 'Door'

Ellie finally found a cat-sized suit of armour

lower parts, particularly the dungeon and basement, are much as when built. The following century saw the building of the Fairy Tower, with its circular wall-hugging staircase. Rory Mor's House was built in 1623. All these buildings were incorporated into the mercifully restrained 'romantic' reconstructions of the nineteenth century.

The cats are slightly apprehensive of going up to the castle, perhaps because they might be called upon to drink a large amount of claret from the Horn of Dunvegan – a feat usually reserved as a rite of passage for a Chief's coming of age, when it must be drained in one draught. (It holds more than a bottle, and the present Chief, John MacLeod, managed it in just under two minutes.) The castle staff are slightly apprehensive too,

lest the cats get their claws into the Fairy Flag of Dunvegan, held in great respect by the Clan, expertly dated at between the fourth and seventh century AD.

Ellie likes the dining room – the ornate silverware compliments her splendid coat – although to her frustration they never hold banquets when she's around. Suits of armour are often a bone of contention with castle cats. They're so big and menacing. But Ellie has found some miniature armour in the study by which she can defiantly sit. Her favourite place of all is the Gun Court, sheltered by the original curtain wall of Leod. As Ellie sits there, taking a line of sight along a cannon barrel, you can almost hear the seals and marauding birds of prey breathe a prayer of thanks for the absence of powder, grapeshot and smoking fuse.

Henry and Harriet

Maybe Harriet took to Castle Fraser because
– unlike many Scottish castles – the only dogs
are stuffed ones, the pets of Colonel Frederick
Mackenzie Fraser, the last of the Frasers to inhabit
the castle.

Henry hightails it for home

When Russell Milne moved with his parents to the West Lodge of Castle Fraser, a superb Scottish baronial tower house built in the sixteenth century, his cat Harriet was a perfectly normal home-loving and pretty tabby. Then things began to change. Harriet, a real homebody, suddenly started to stay away, first for a few days, then for a month or more, and finally for ever.

Rumours reached them of a cat like Harriet being seen more and more regularly in and around the castle. Harriet seems simply to have decided that she preferred the castle to her very pleasant, caring home. Her quiet invasion was only discovered when Eric Wilkinson, the Property Manager, and his wife Ann, saw the spectral figure of a cat, slinking silently down a spiral stone staircase at dusk (a far more agreeable ghostly event than the persistently reappearing bloodstains said to

mark the scene of a gruesome murder in the Green Room).

It was Harriet's fondness for jam that brought her into the open. She emerged in the kitchen, where she would usually be found daintily licking her favourite delicacy off a part-made sandwich.

Russell and his mother Karen continued to raid the castle in a series of vain attempts to get Harriet home, to no avail. By now she had adopted the gardeners and their potting shed where she often spent a warm night near heated plant propagators. She also had her acolyte, in the form of a newly-arrived cat called Henry, living with Head Gardener, Iain Davies, his wife Sharon, and their children Jack and Annie.

Despite Iain's status, Henry plays second fiddle to Harriet. She permits him only to trail after her at a

Keeping a low profile

Waiting in vain for Harriet

respectable distance, while she does the hunting. Woe betide Henry if he tries to rival her efforts, although he is permitted to polish off the rabbits that she despatches with legendary prowess. At mealtimes Harriet appears at Iain's cottage, tucking in heartily while Henry looks mildly on waiting for whatever she deigns to leave.

Fear can be a great leveller. Sometimes the cats meet a wild cat in the surrounding woods, at which point both beat a hasty retreat – Harriet to the castle gatehouse, Henry to his cottage. Henry is certainly not permitted to go near the castle. In fact he gets a good cuff round the ears if he even points in that direction. Harriet keeps for herself the kitchen visits and the chance of superb haggis; Eric and Ann's son, Jamie, has an extremely comfortable bed; there are roaring log fires during the winter in the Great Hall; a squint hole over-

looks the Great Hall from the Priest's Room, and allows Harriet to see if there are any leftovers after a social gathering. This brazen cat even walks with Iain and Sharon Davies' children to the school bus.

Poor Henry is an amiable chap but still a bit wide-eyed. Shortly after arriving at Castle Fraser, he was chased up a tree by an irate ram, where he spent a cold, uncomfortable and wind-tossed night before being rescued by Iain and Sharon. At present the castle overawes him, but he's growing fast and may soon give as good as he gets.

As for Russell, he has seen that Harriet is happy, and has acquired a new kitten, who had to give a paw-printed undertaking not to be out of the house for more than ten minutes at a time. I can well understand. In two days of hunting high and low, through the castle, gardens and surrounding woods, I never did find Harriet.

Sophie and Runcie

Sophie and Runcie boast their own sallyport,
designed and constructed to traditional medieval
defensive principles.

Runcie and Sophie: cats couchant

Sophie: the castle chatelaine

Fires blaze especially for the Penhow cats

Well, perhaps sallyport is a bit fanciful, but Stephen Weeks, film maker, writer, conservationist and fond owner of Sophie and Runcie, found a medieval drain in the seven-foot thick walls of the Norman keep which now houses his kitchen. A leather flap on the inside keeps out the draughts, and the outer exit is now a veritable cat's gatehouse, a secret exit out of which the cats can surprise unwelcome visitors whilst being almost impregnable to invaders.

The kitchen doubles as a garrison mess for Runcie and Sophie, who spend a fair amount of time curled up as close to the stove as is possible without being casseroled, whilst still being in earshot of the drawbridge and their own egress.

Norman in origin, Penhow stands defiantly on an exposed hillock, and was one of a chain of knights' castles intended to protect outlying farms, serving as an early warning post for any Welsh uprising. Stephen Weeks has been restoring the castle for twenty-three years, and the oldest parts of the castle – the keep, gatehouse and Great Hall – are a fascinating reminder of the castle's past. The border winds may blow cold, but the castle cats at Penhow have the consolation of knowing that there is a roaring fire in many of the massive stone fireplaces, lit specifically – they presume – for their comfort.

The first of Stephen's castle cats, Percy, came from a London animal rescue centre, as did the second – Augustus, who unfortunately did not survive long. Percy, being a real Londoner, was not impressed with Penhow's wild position and thought nothing of its strategic advantages. Thinking longingly of those tantalizingly smelly London pavements, he adopted the paved courtyard, comfortingly enclosed by a thick stone curtain wall – complete with walkways, lookout

On guard in the Great Hall

points and battlements – a sort of medieval adventure playground for cats. As a bit of a playboy, he was a miserable hunter. The only mouse he ever caught was already in a trap. Augustus, on the other hand, was a more godly cat, regularly visiting the nearby church, itself equipped with arrow slits.

Tufton and Alice Springs followed, but it was Percy who survived to assume responsibility for initiating Sophie and Runcie, the present incumbents. Sophie is a foundling, who came back with Stephen and Percy from a local vet's. Percy straightaway set about teaching Sophie the proper bearing for a castle cat, allowing her to strike the impressive poses at the far side of the drawbridge in the wind, while he ensconced himself in the shelter of the courtyard, reminiscing about happy London nights of howling, street fights and general hell-raising.

When Percy died, a new companion for Sophie was found at Canterbury Cathedral – Runcie, named after a former Archbishop. Runcie's mother, Manhattan, had blotted her copybook at the cathedral when she ran across the altar during a service, pausing in horror at the centre as it suddenly dawned that her antics were being observed by a huge silent congregation and gathering of ecclesiastical dignitaries. Her offspring were accordingly banished. Runcie hasn't quite shaken off his cathedral cat background, and follows Augustus in going to the occasional service in the nearby church.

By the time of Runcie's arrival Sophie had taken on the demeanour of castle chatelaine, and to this day the two cats can be heard vigorously discussing their respective positions in the castle hierarchy. However, when faced with the threat of outside intervention, both cats man their defensive positions with military precision. It took Sophie a little while to work them out, as a visitor observed when he saw the wriggling backquarters of a cat protruding out of a hole in the battlements.

Sophie and Runcie yearn for the Christmas evenings at Penhow, when all the fires blaze, and they can listen to carols whilst artfully relieving visitors of mince pies. They also enjoy sabotaging the frequent educational visits of schoolchildren, organized by Stephen's partner Kathleen who runs the castle. Many a teacher has had to struggle to regain the attention of children in the Great Hall who would much rather watch two black cats sitting disdainfully on the sixteenth-century High Seat next to a sign saying 'Please don't sit here' than listen to an historical exposition.

Acknowledgements

The author and publisher would like to thank the following for their help
and cooperation in making this book possible:

Jill Hammond, Kay Hayward and Mrs Robinson, BERKELEY CASTLE
James and The Hon. Sarah Hervey-Bathurst, EASTNOR CASTLE
Doug Goodyer, HEVER CASTLE
Peter Frost-Pennington and family, MUNCASTER CASTLE
Sir Thomas Ingilby and Colin Claydon, RIPLEY CASTLE
Commander and Mrs Saunders Watson, ROCKINGHAM CASTLE
Richard Topham, ST MICHAEL'S MOUNT
Colonel and Mrs Hamish Mackinlay, THE TOWER OF LONDON
Mrs Sylvia Stephens and Major General Downward CB DSO DFC, WINDSOR CASTLE

Yvonne Acheson and Kay Bowman, BUNRATTY CASTLE
Constance Heavey-Alagna and Bridget Vance, CHARLEVILLE FOREST CASTLE
Brian and Elyse Thompson, CLOGHAN CASTLE
Jonathan and Betty Sykes and family, SPRINGFIELD CASTLE
Mr and Mrs Thomas Pakenham, TULLYNALLY CASTLE

Nigel Price, Clare Reaney and Mrs Olive Raymond, BRODICK CASTLE
William and Marigold Bowman and Iain Crisp, CRATHES CASTLE
Christopher and Sarah Whealing, and Alistair Lord Strathnaver, DUNROBIN CASTLE
John MacLeod and John Lambert and family, DUNVEGAN CASTLE
Eric and Ann Wilkinson, Russell Milne and Iain and Sharon Davies, CASTLE FRASER

Stephen Weeks, PENHOW CASTLE

The National Trust for Scotland for the line drawings of Brodick Castle, Crathes Castle and Castle Fraser.
David Hearn for the line drawings of Berkeley Castle, Eastnor Castle, St Michael's Mount and Windsor Castle.
Stephen Weeks for the line drawing of Penhow Castle.

Unless otherwise stated, the line drawings of the castles
are reproduced by permission of the castle owners.